The Lake

Lily Richardson

It is spring.
Wildflowers bloom near the lake.

People sail on the lake.

It is summer.
Birds drink from the lake.

People swim in the lake.

It is **fall**.
The trees near the lake change color.

People fish in the lake.

It is **winter**.
The lake freezes over.

People skate on the lake.